Machines at Work

Icebreakers

by Cari Meister

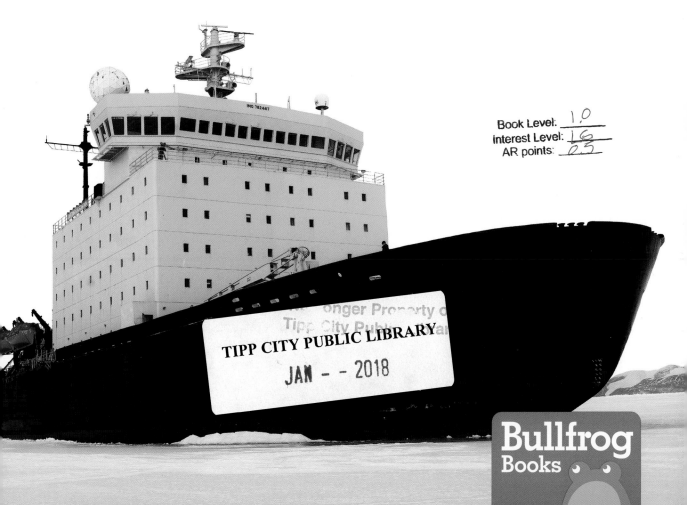

Book Level: 1.0
Interest Level: LG
AR points: 0.5

onger Property o
Tipp City Pub

TIPP CITY PUBLIC LIBRARY

JAN - - 2018

Bullfrog
Books

Ideas for Parents and Teachers

Bullfrog Books let children practice reading informational text at the earliest reading levels. Repetition, familiar words, and photo labels support early readers.

Before Reading

- Discuss the cover photo. What does it tell them?

- Look at the picture glossary together. Read and discuss the words.

Read the Book

- "Walk" through the book and look at the photos. Let the child ask questions. Point out the photo labels.

- Read the book to the child, or have him or her read independently.

After Reading

- Prompt the child to think more. Ask: Have you ever seen an icebreaker? Was it working?

Bullfrog Books are published by Jump!
5357 Penn Avenue South
Minneapolis, MN 55419
www.jumplibrary.com

Copyright © 2017 Jump! International copyright reserved in all countries. No part of this book may be reproduced in any form without written permission from the publisher.

Library of Congress Cataloging-in-Publication Data

Names: Meister, Cari, author.
Title: Icebreakers / by Cari Meister.
Other titles: Bullfrog books. Machines at work.
Description: Minneapolis, MN: Jump!, Inc. [2017]
Series: Bullfrog books. Machines at work
Audience: Ages 5–8. | Audience: K to grade 3.
Identifiers: LCCN 2016002943 (print)
LCCN 2016006040 (ebook)
ISBN 9781620313688 (hardcover: alk. paper)
ISBN 9781620314869 (paperback)
ISBN 9781624964152 (ebook)
Subjects: LCSH: Icebreakers (Ships)—
Juvenile literature.
Classification: LCC VM451.M45 2017 (print)
LCC VM451 (ebook) | DDC 623.82/8—dc23
LC record available at http://lccn.loc.gov/2016002943

Editor: Jenny Fretland VanVoorst
Series Designer: Ellen Huber
Book Designer: Leah Sanders
Photo Researcher: Leah Sanders

Photo Credits: All photos by Shutterstock except: Alamy, 6–7; Corbis, cover; Dreamstime, 17, 20–21; Getty, 5, 10–11, 13; SuperStock, 1, 8–9, 14–15, 22.

Printed in the United States of America at Corporate Graphics in North Mankato, Minnesota.

Table of Contents

Icebreakers at Work

Oh, no! Look.

A ship is stuck in the ice.

Don't worry.

Here comes an icebreaker.

hull

It can help.

It has a strong hull.

The bow goes up on the ice.

It pushes down on the ice.

The boat is heavy.

The ice breaks.

The big engines rev.

The thick propellers spin.

The big boat pushes.

The ice chunks move.

The boat makes a path.

The stuck ship is free!

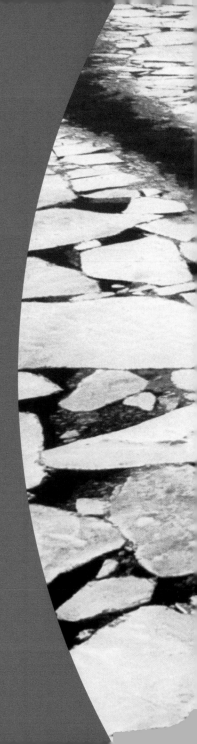

People need oil for fuel.

A tanker has oil.

But the lake is ice.

The tanker cannot move.

It is OK.

Here comes
an icebreaker!

It breaks the ice.

It pushes the ice.

Now the tanker can go.

Good work!

IMO 6705937

LOUIS S. ST-LAURENT

Canada

Parts of an Icebreaker

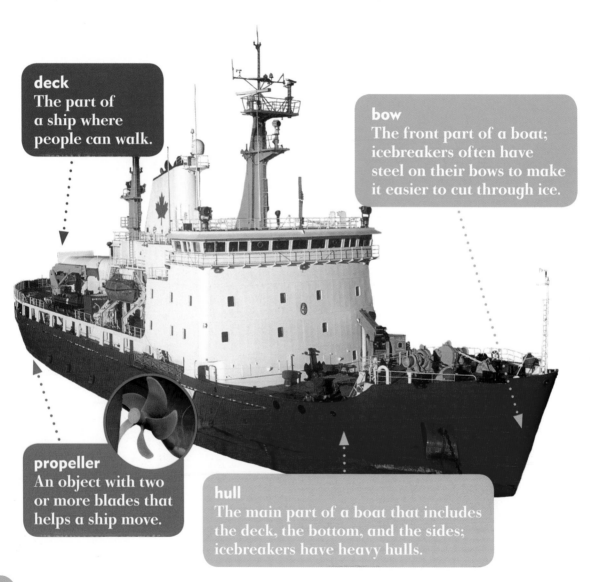

deck
The part of a ship where people can walk.

bow
The front part of a boat; icebreakers often have steel on their bows to make it easier to cut through ice.

propeller
An object with two or more blades that helps a ship move.

hull
The main part of a boat that includes the deck, the bottom, and the sides; icebreakers have heavy hulls.

Picture Glossary

fuel
A material, like gasoline, that is burned to make heat.

rev
To make an engine work harder or quicker.

oil
A black liquid that comes from the ground and is used as fuel.

tanker
A ship that carries liquids.

Index

To Learn More

Learning more is as easy as 1, 2, 3.

1) Go to www.factsurfer.com

2) Enter "icebreakers" into the search box.

3) Click the "Surf" button to see a list of websites.

With factsurfer.com, finding more information is just a click away.

No Longer Property of
Tipp City Public Library